We ChOse You

Ane B. Burke

ISBN 979-8-88616-667-5 (paperback)
ISBN 979-8-89043-004-5 (hardcover)
ISBN 979-8-88616-668-2 (digital)

Christian Faith Publishing
832 Park Avenue
Meadville, PA 16335
www.christianfaithpublishing.com

Printed in the United States of America

God's heart for orphans and adoption is displayed throughout the Old and New Testaments. Adoption is woven through scripture and serves to not only strengthen our faith but also to encourage us as we meet the needs of the precious children.

Matthew 1:18

In the New Testament, Jesus was conceived through the Holy Spirit and was adopted by his mother's husband. Joseph took Jesus as his own child, and along with Mary, they raised a son who changed the course of history.

To the love of my life—my husband, John—and my lifelong mentor—my mother, Clydean—thank you for your encouragement and love. I cherish, love, and admire you both.

It has been a privilege to glorify our Lord and Savior, Jesus Christ.

To my special friend Jessica Garst for all your fabulous input and talent. I love ya.

God is Love

God is Love

The wonderful world of *God* tells us that Jesus was adopted by his mother's husband, Joseph. Joseph loved Jesus as his own child, and together, this *raised Jesus—the Savior of the World*, who would change the course of history. God shows us that being *adopted* is a wonderful and beautiful part of life.

Wow, Michael! Isn't it exciting that Jesus *was* adopted j*ust like you?*

Before you came into my life, I would often dream about my younger years as a *mommy*. I remember all the fun times and laughter I cherished with your brother, Willie. Oh, that seems so long ago. We played games, rode bikes, and slept in tents on the floor. Such fun memories for me, and now he is grown with kids of his own!

I love being a mom, and I still have so much love to give! When I ask, "Is there a child out there that would need or even want a loving mom like me?"

I am getting older and even a bit slower, but still I ask, "Is there a child that would want to love a mom like me?"

Yes, I can take a test, sing a song, and dance a jig.

I can bake a cake or make a bed—oh, these precious thoughts continue to dance in my head.

I know that I am older. Yet again, a mother I want to be. If there is a child out there needing love, please, dear God, send him to me.

God has such magnificent plans for our lives. He knows the desires of our hearts.

He knew he would give me a son in my youth, and that later he would again bless me with yet another son—then came *you!*

Oh, Michael, I knew from the first moment I looked at your beautiful little face and your dancing, sparkling eyes smiling back at me that I wanted with all my heart to be your mom.

Your daddy and I chose *you!*

You were given our name and our home once again rang with laughter, smiles, and an abundance of joy.

Our son, *Michael.*

Our blessed dream comes true.

Our little bundle of *joy.*

You sweet Michael have given our lives new meaning. The time you skinned your knees, the nights you had a fever, the special way you laugh when your daddy tickles you, the way you make us feel when you lavish us with your hugs—we have such a deep love for our *sweet, precious boy!*

The years pass, and I watch you grow! My precious Michael, I sometimes wonder if you will ever understand that my heart is heavy. It hurts me that I am unable to race you or ride a bike down the street or turn a cartwheel.

However, Michael, let me tell you *what I can and will do.* I will prepare yummy meals you will so enjoy eating and bake your favorite cookies for you and your friends!

I'll teach you about birds and their love songs and how to garden, craft, and roast marshmallows over an open campfire. I'll watch those scary movies while hiding under a blanket. I'll eat popcorn, and count the stars with you.

Together we'll catch

lightning bugs, play in the creek,
and drive the golf cart all around.

I'll be your chef, your taxi, and your teacher. I'll be your nurse and a great listener and, of course, your biggest *fan*. I'll be here for you if ever you have a broken heart. Most importantly, my son, I'll teach you the love of *God* and disciple you just the same.

I'll teach you to *love* others with compassion and a giving heart.

I'll watch you with your daddy—your own Papa Bear! He'll teach you to ride a bike, drive a car, and play golf. He will love, provide, and protect you.

You'll ride on his shoulders, catch frogs from the creek and bugs in the grass, and love you with all of his heart. Oh, I pray you'll have his wit, but most importantly, he will instruct you in the ways of the Lord.

Oh, son of mine, you will also have the love of your grandmother.

She'll fix your boo-boos and let you stay up all night. You two will go for long walks and play board games, and she'll laugh at your silly sounds. Oh, we'll have so much fun growing up in our own unique way with school, games, and super vacations.

Together we will sit and listen to the thunder until the storm goes away and the rainbow covers the earth. The birds will be singing, the dog will continue barking, and the butterflies will flutter on the flowers.

My sweet Michael, have you gazed at a *rainbow* and considered all its colors?

Oh, let's do it. Let me tell you how I see *you* in the *rainbow*!

The first color is blue. Blue, like the sky, reminds me of your sparkling greyish-blue eyes.

Red is next. This color represents the love in my heart I have for you—the tie that binds us.

Indigo represents honor and wisdom. I pray you'll grow blessed with these traits.

Green displays your abundance of energy, hope, and future growth.

Violet reminds me that you are precious in the sight of God.

Orange is the happiness and laughter that follow you wherever you go.

Yellow shouts the joy I see in your heart and soul.

This is our special journey together!

We were *adopted* together as a family!

You will always be our child, and we will always be your parents.

We *love* you, Michael!

We chose you.

About the Author

After spending most of her life in Arkansas, Ane now resides in Missouri. She shares her love of farm life with her husband, John Clydean, her mother, and her son Michael. Ane is also the mother of Willie, his wife, Haley (her daughter-in-love), and her three beautiful grandloves—Reese, Quinn, and Will E. We can't forget the three paw babies—Cash, Cari, and Riley. Ane enjoys gardening, cooking, writing, creating jewelry, playing guitar with hubby, John, and also laughing and enjoying time with her mother. Ane's education includes law, home building, and administrative long-term health care. Ane loves the Lord, so it was important when they adopted Michael that he understands how loved he is by the family.

Realizing how many seniors were adopting children or raising their grandchildren, Ane knew it was important for Michael and other adopted children to understand how special it is to be adopted. Ephesians 1:5 says that God decided in advance to adopt us into his own family by bringing us to himself through Jesus Christ. This is what he wanted to do, and it gave him great pleasure.

Being an older parent, Ane understands the different challenges that come with raising children as a senior versus raising children in their twenties, thirties, or forties. Ane hopes this series of *We Chose You* will help other adopted children and more mature parents understand this blessing and learn to enjoy, laugh, and maybe even cry, but mostly cherish and enjoy this special time of life. Ane understands that priorities may have changed and disciplining may not be what it once was; but the fun, the laughter, and the memories are so worth every minute of every day. Thank you, Lord Jesus, for trusting us with your precious child. It truly is a joy being an older, adoptive parent.